Tevi Woehl

MANDALA

A Coloring Book

Design and layout for cover and text: © 2019 by Tevi Woehl Studio

Printed in the United States of America
First Printing November 2019

ISBN-13: 978-0-9987588-3-1

Visit us online at www.teviwoehl.com

This book belongs to

Use This Page To Test Your Colors

Use This Page To Test Your Colors

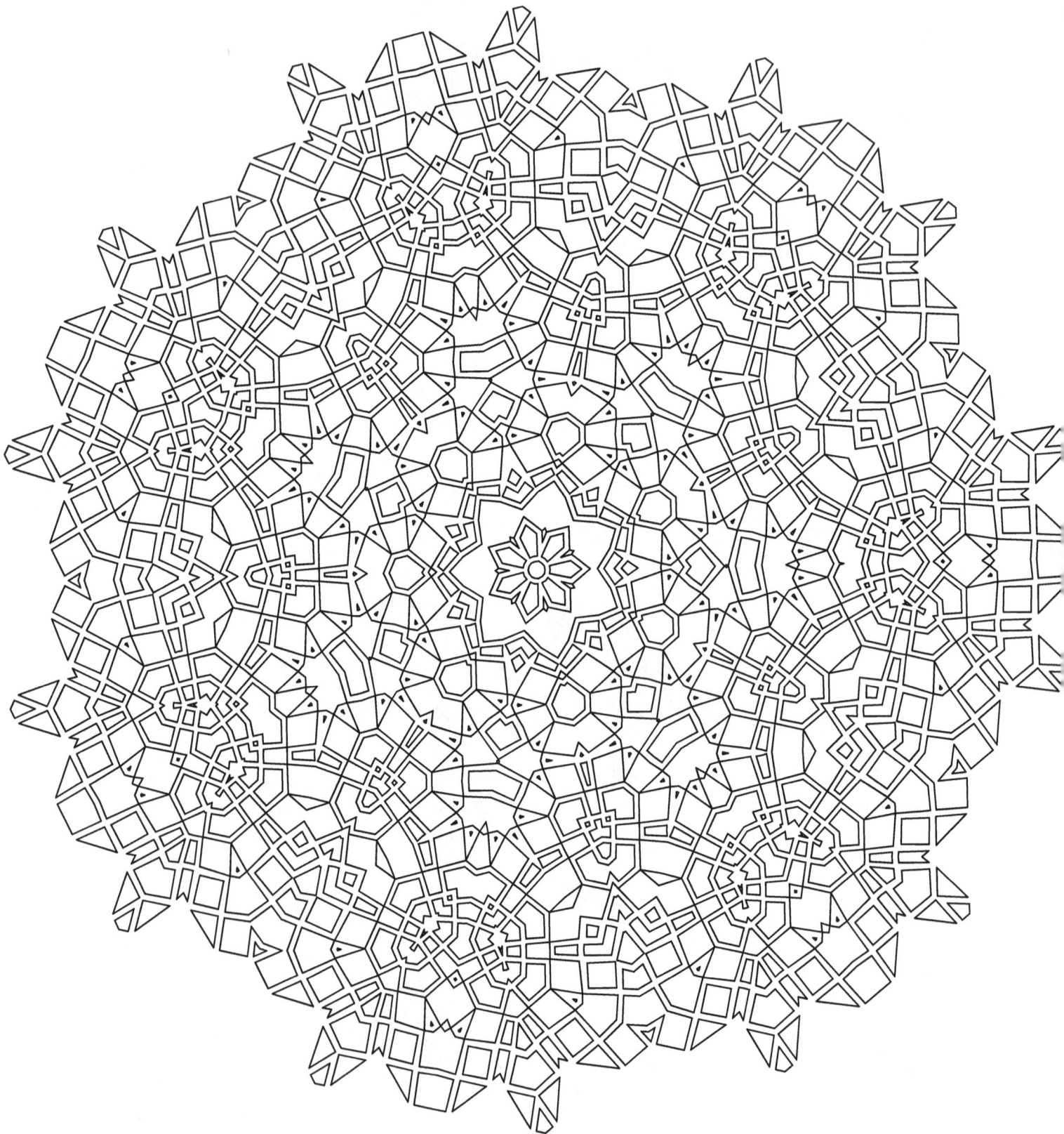

Use This Page To Test Your Colors

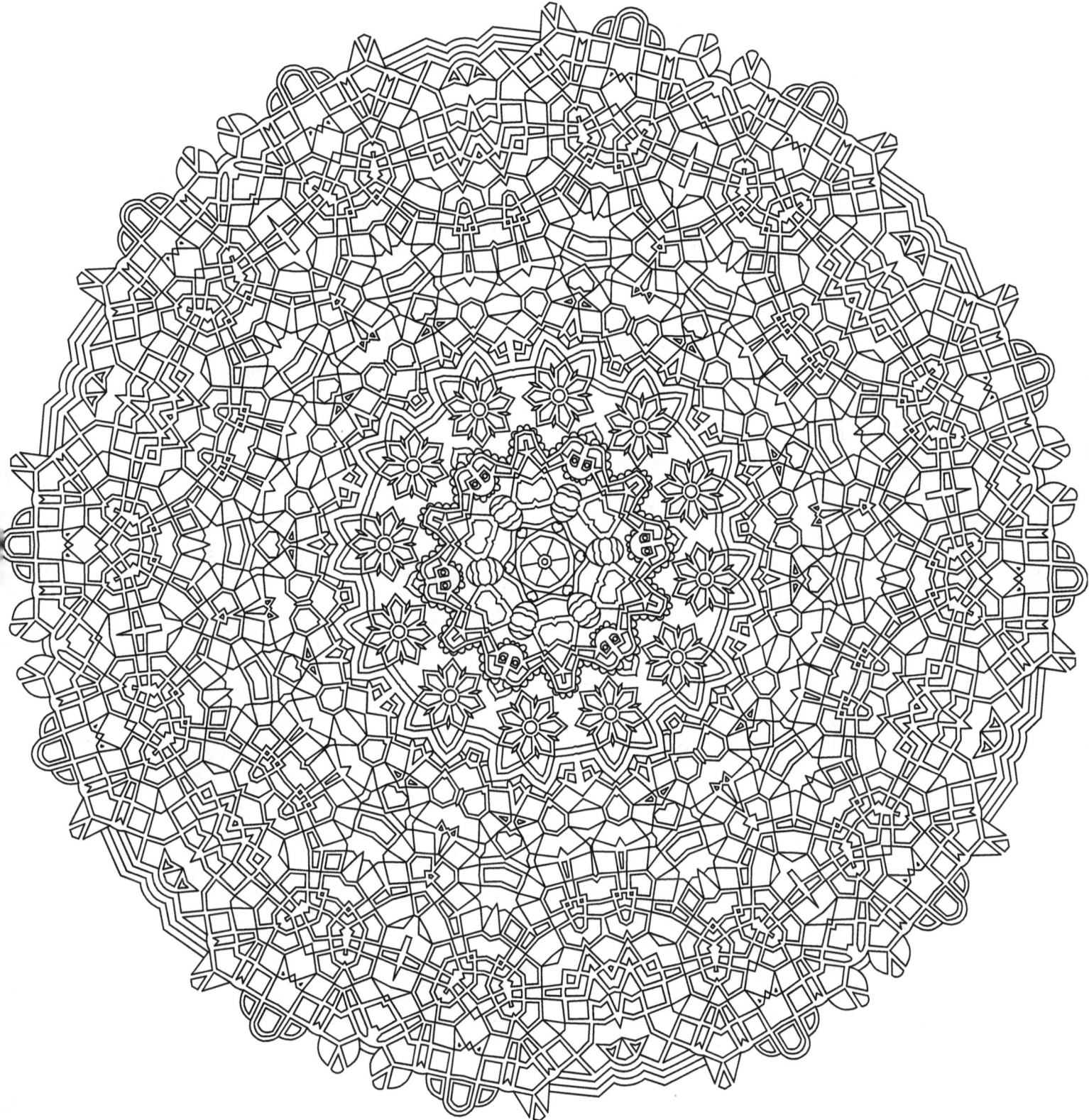

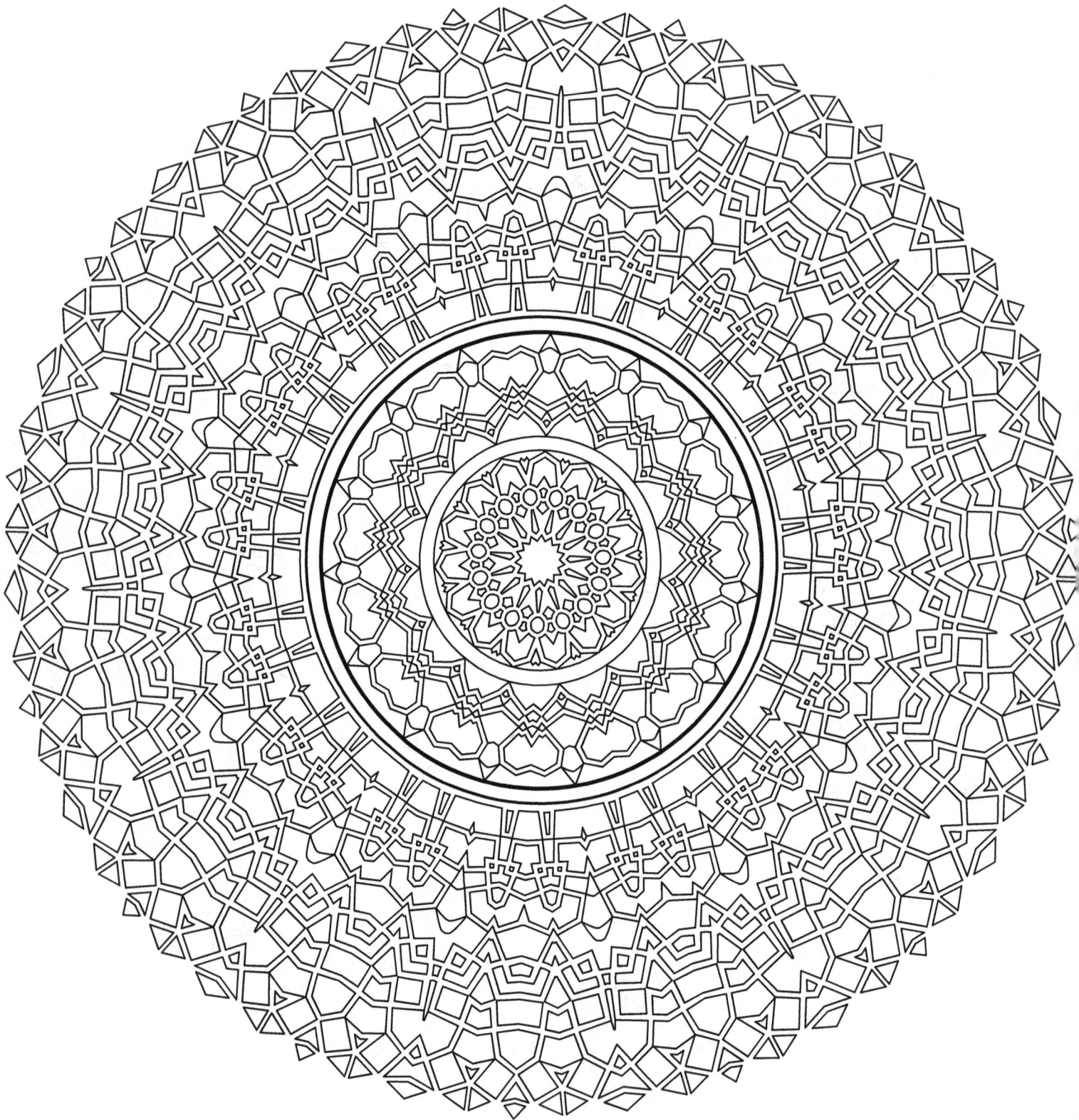

Use This Page To Test Your Colors

Also by Tevi Woehl

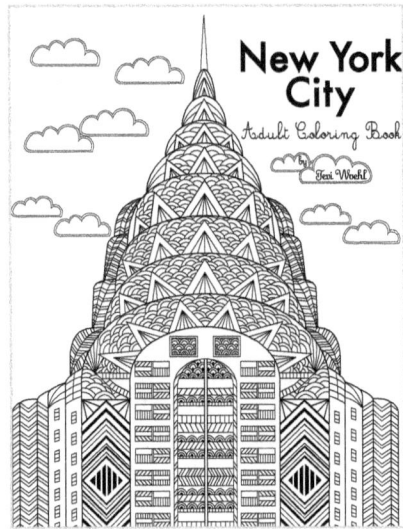

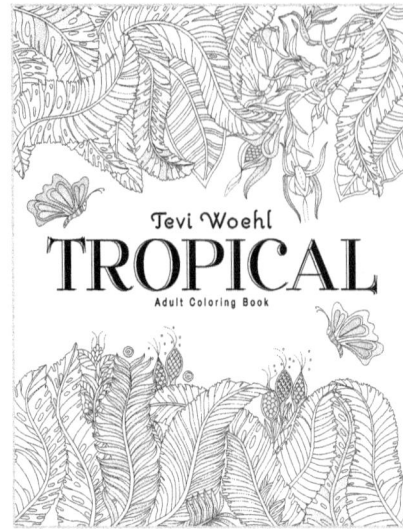

We would love to hear from you! E-mail your thoughts and questions to *twoehlstudio@gmail.com*. If you like to share your coloring pages, e-mail your lovely work and we will post it in our blog. Join our mailing list at *www.teviwoehl.com* to get updates, news, and a chance to win great giveaways and freebies!

Let's See Your Coloring Pages!
@teviwoehlstudio